THIS BOOK

BELONG TO

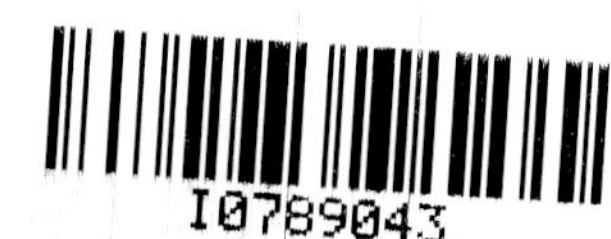

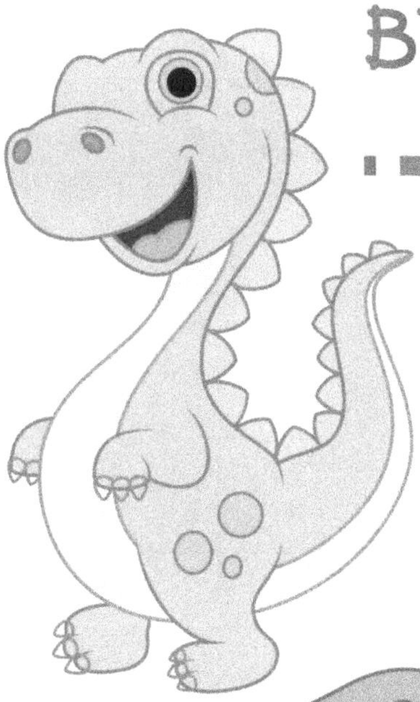

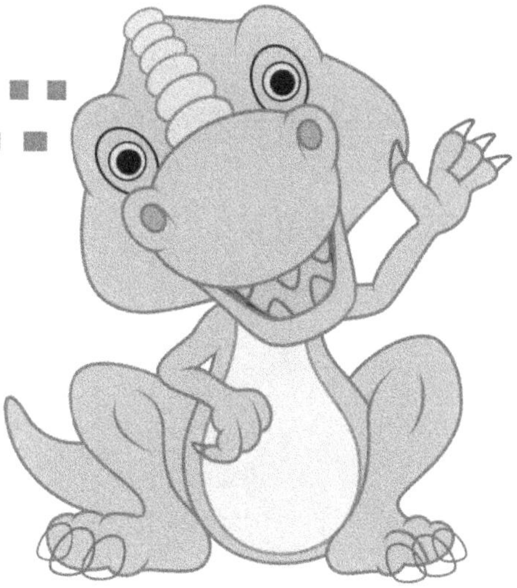

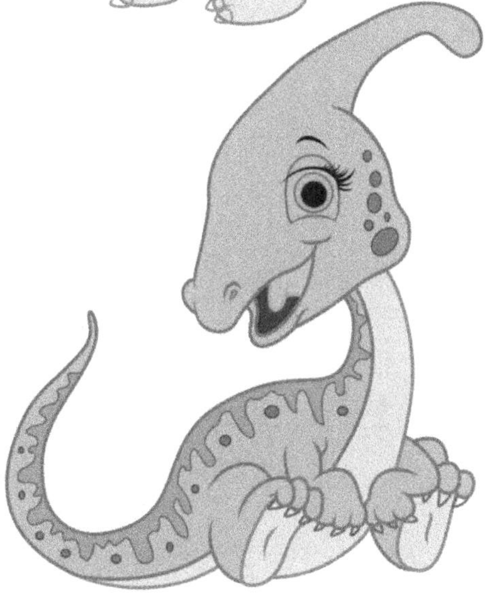

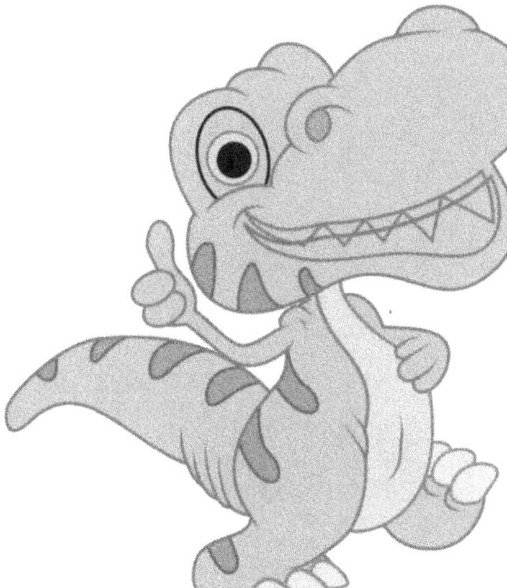

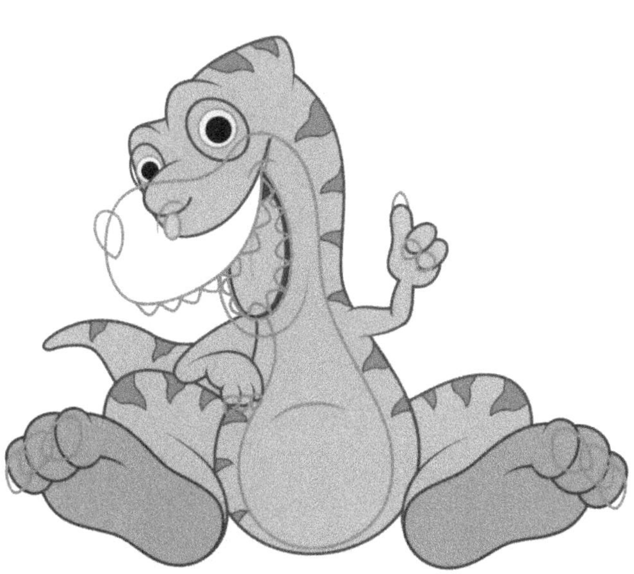

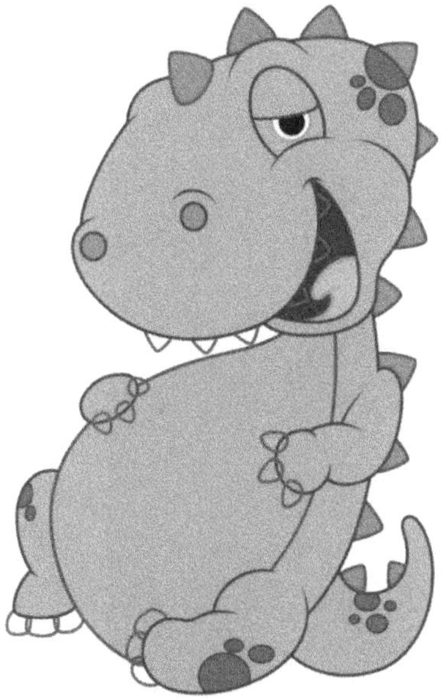

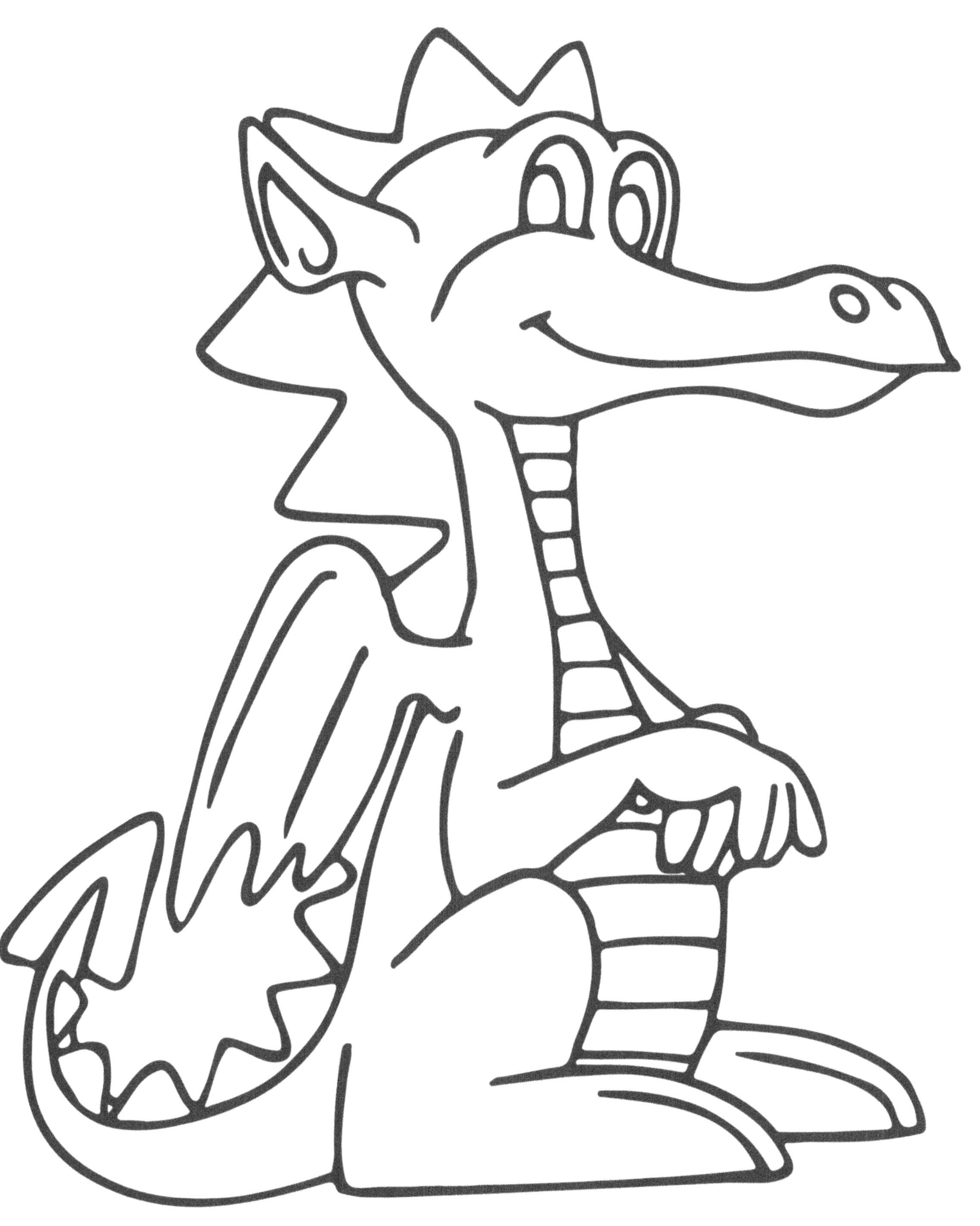

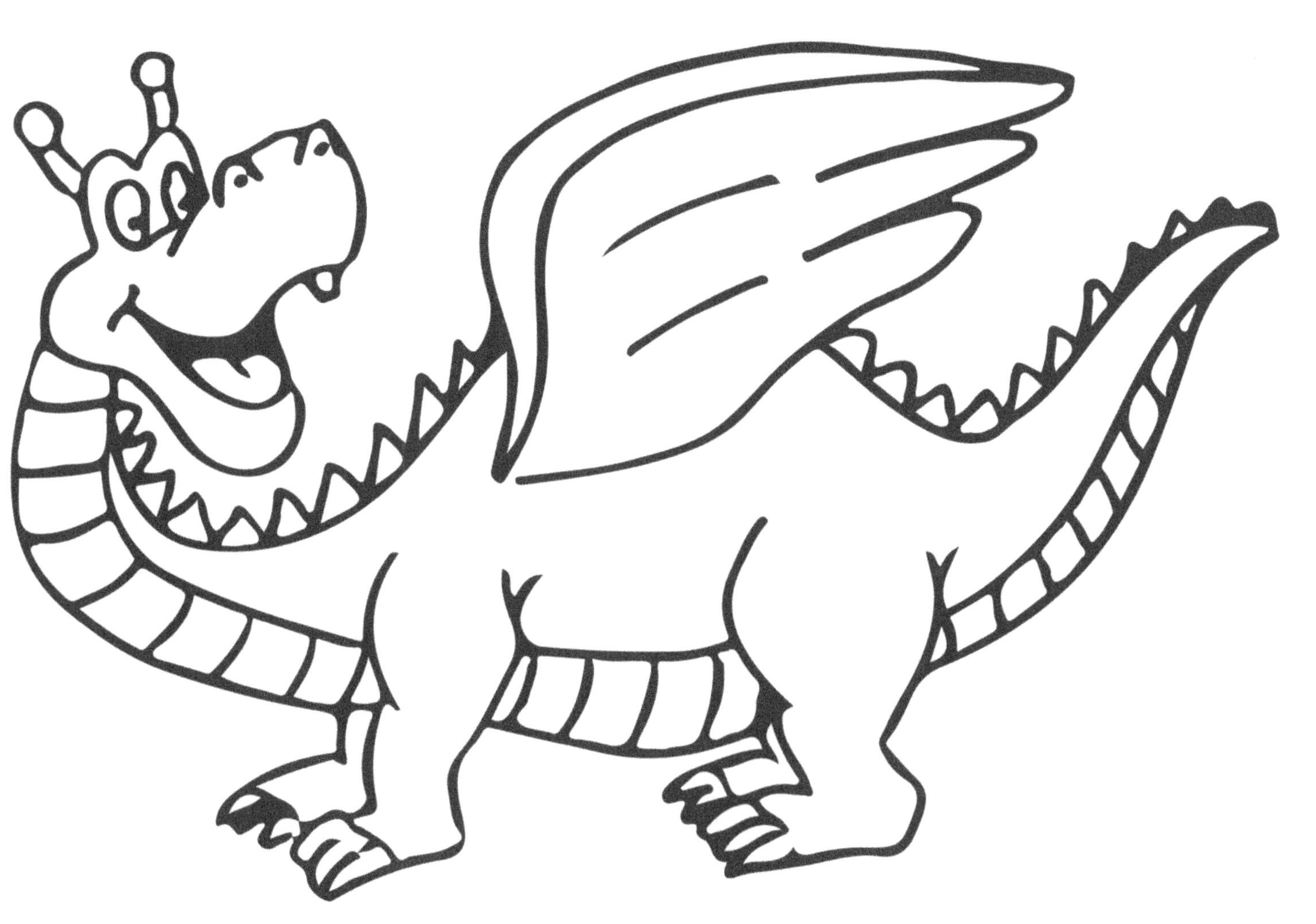

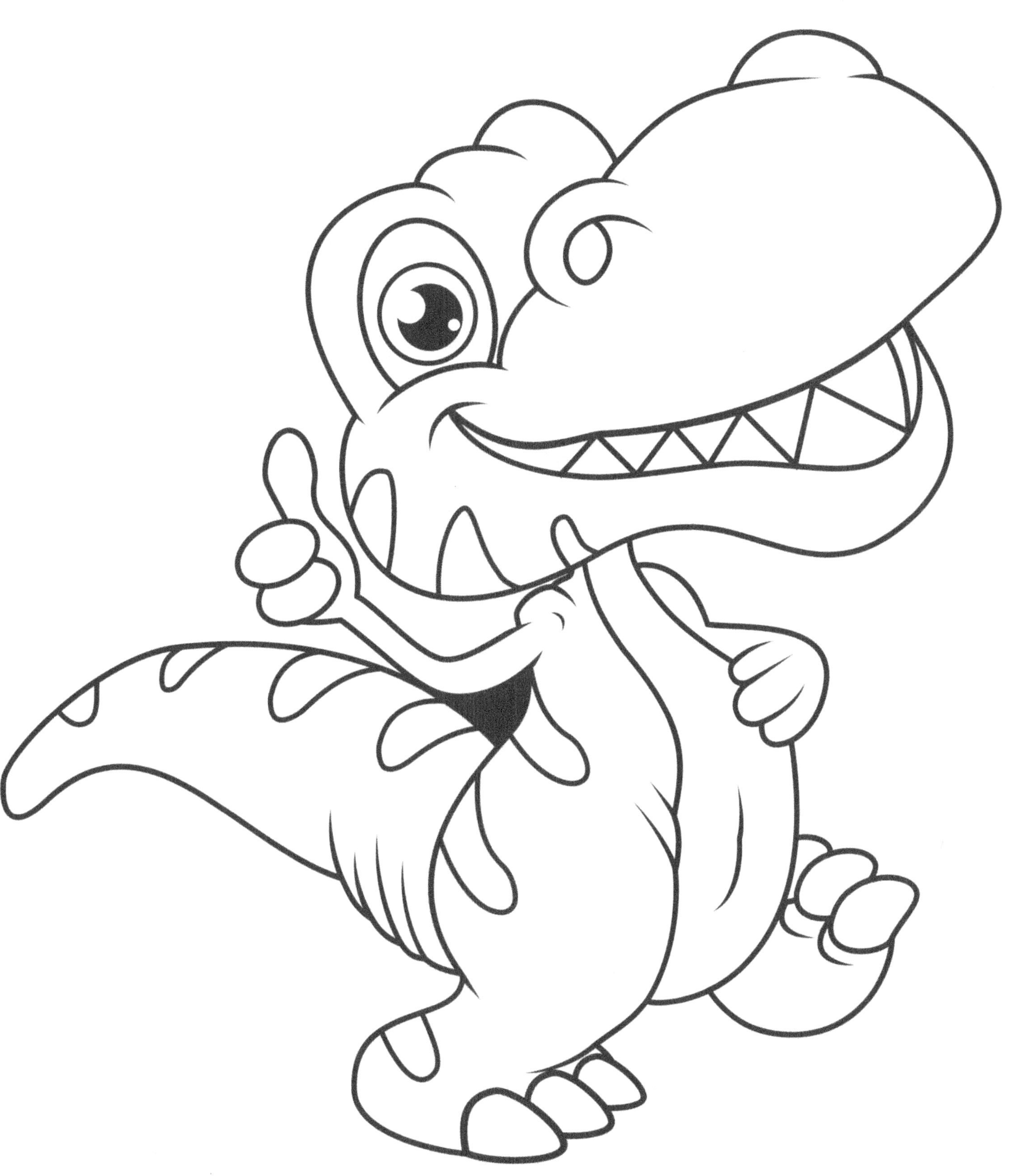

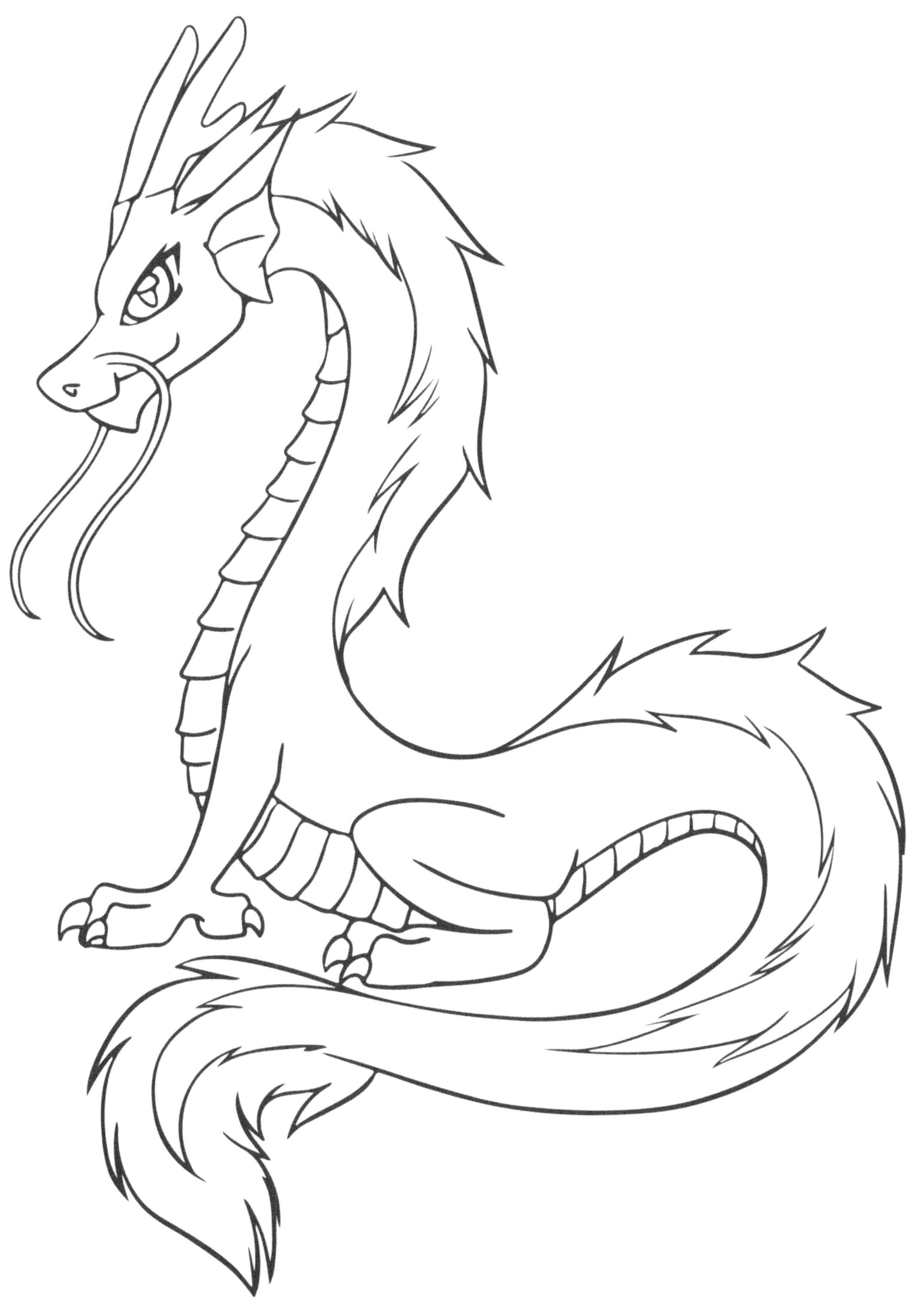

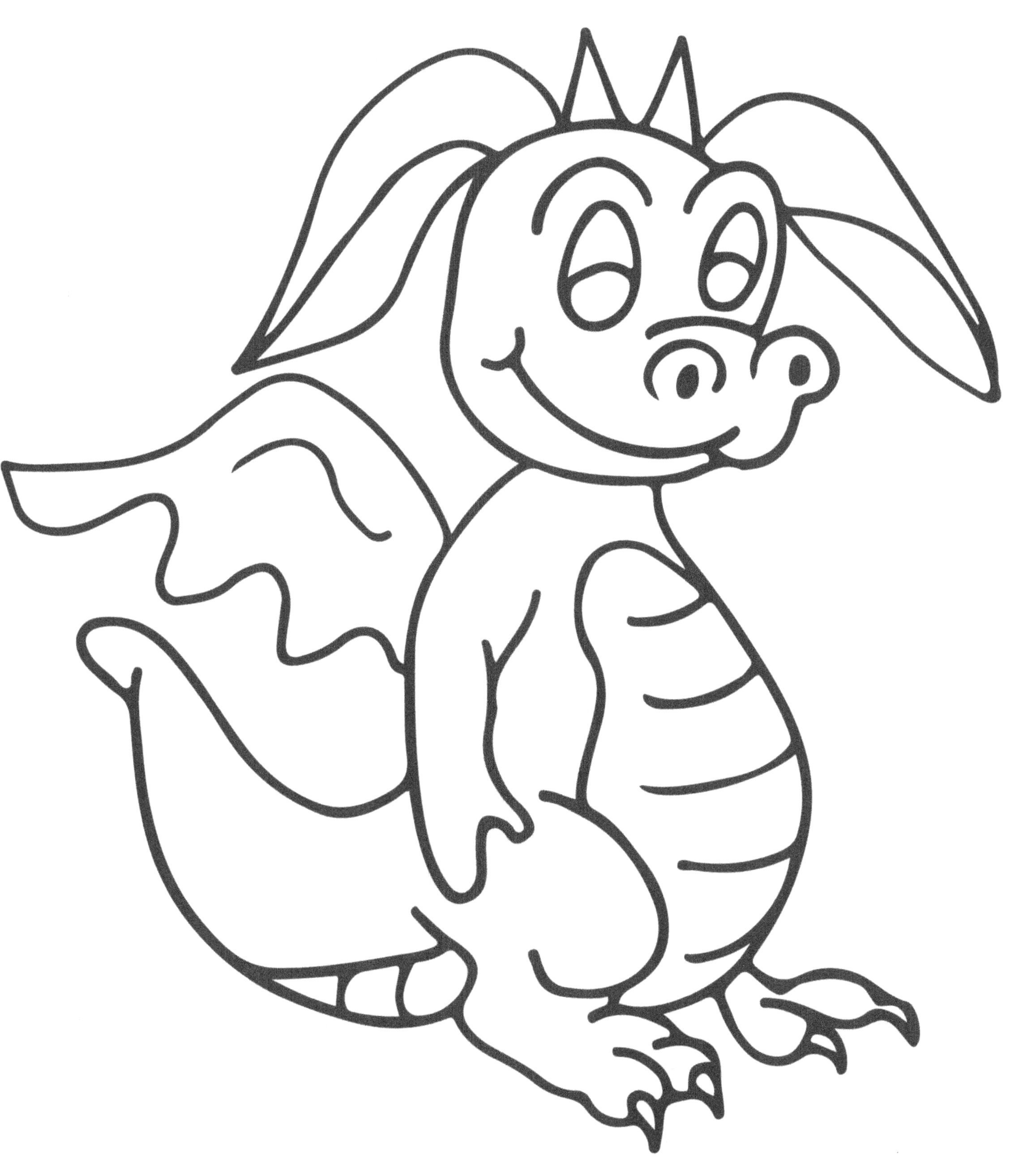

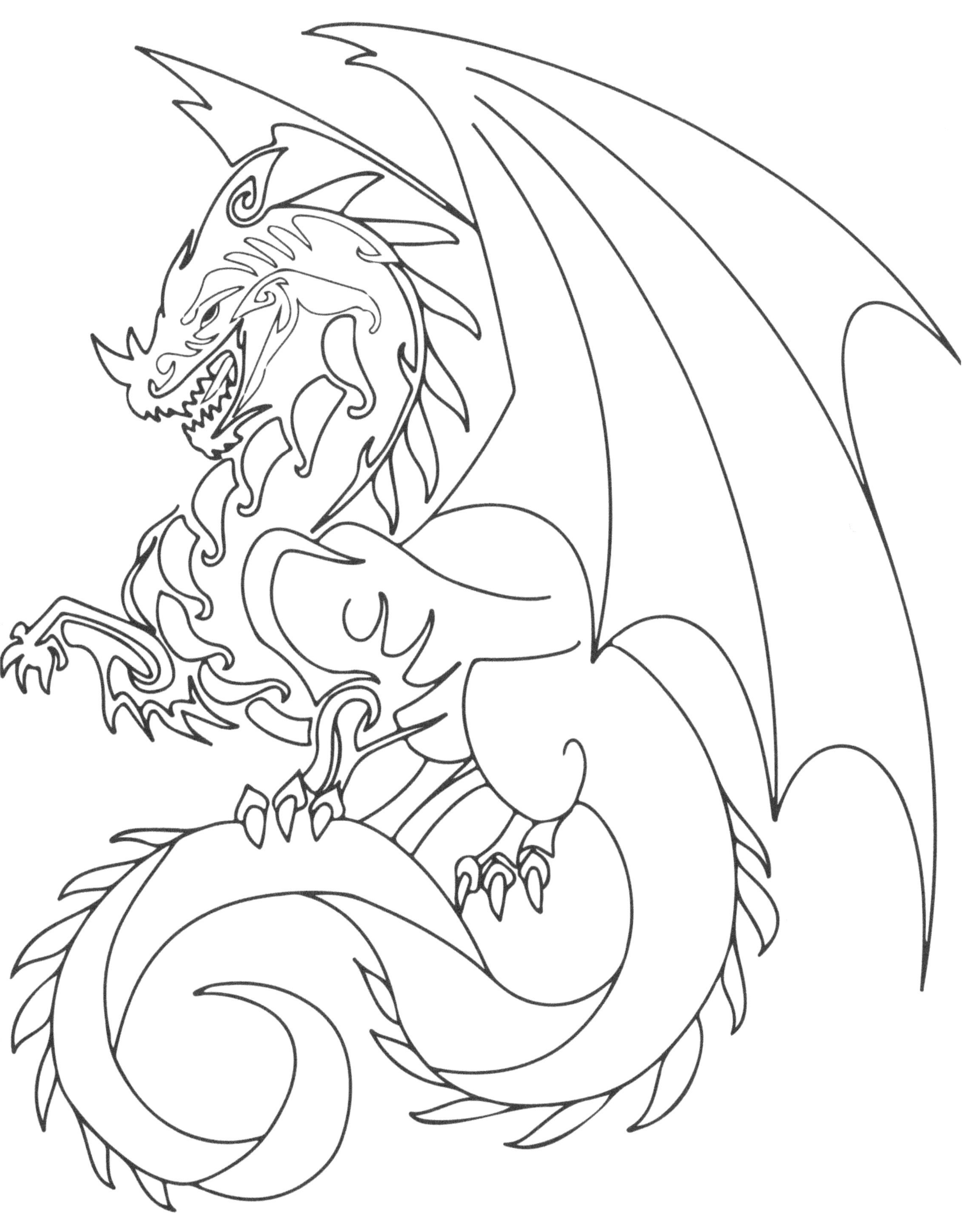

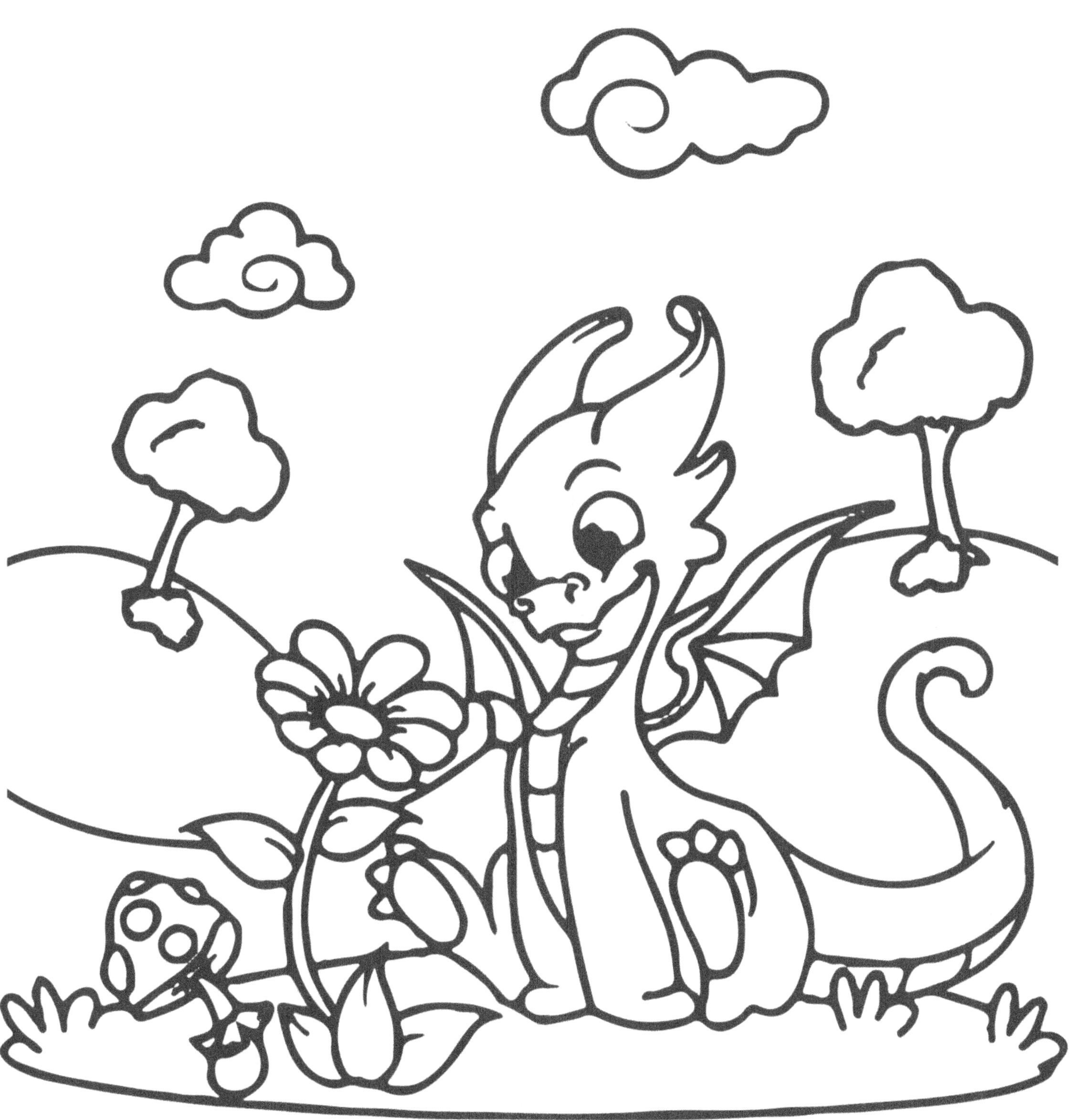

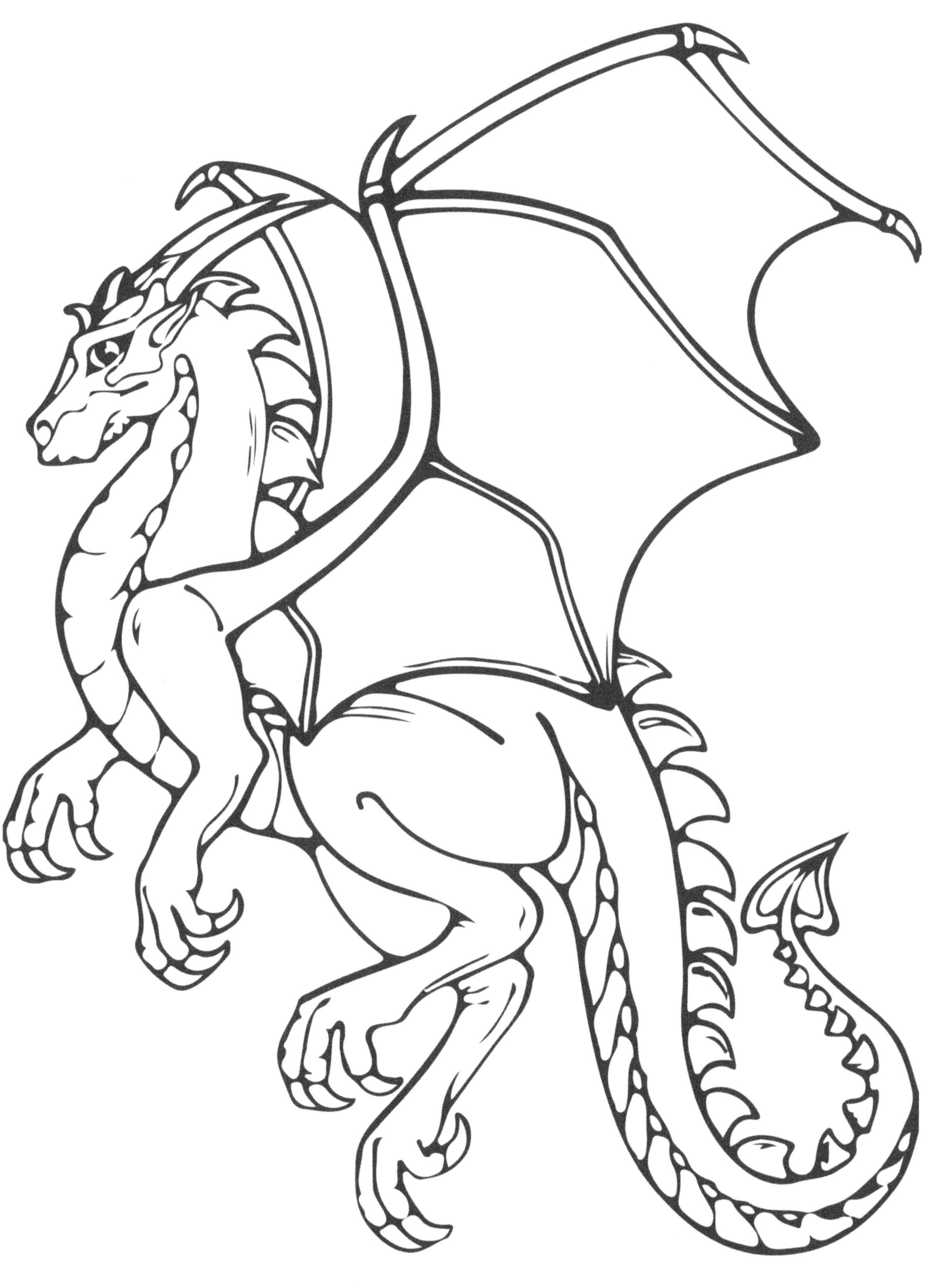

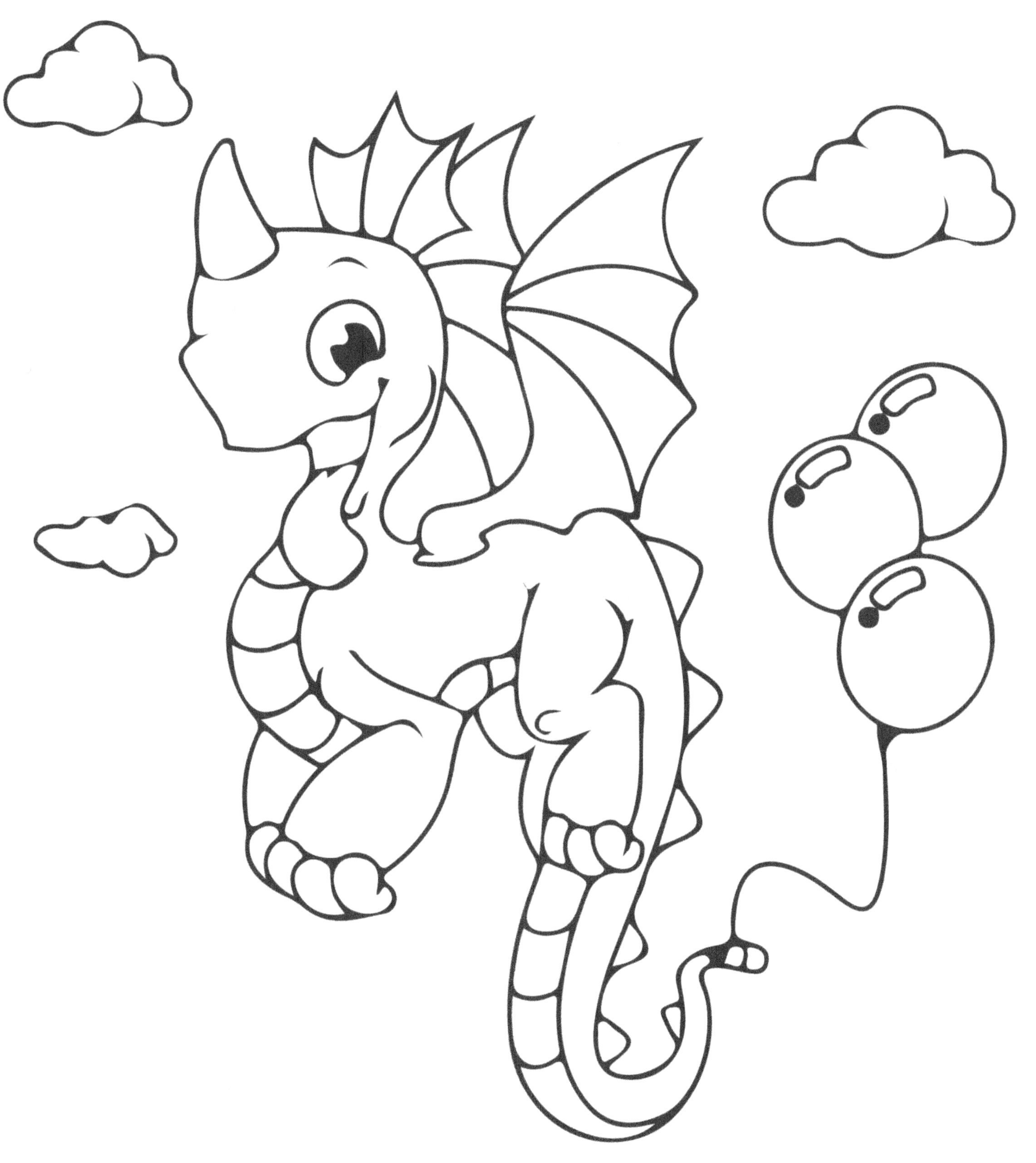

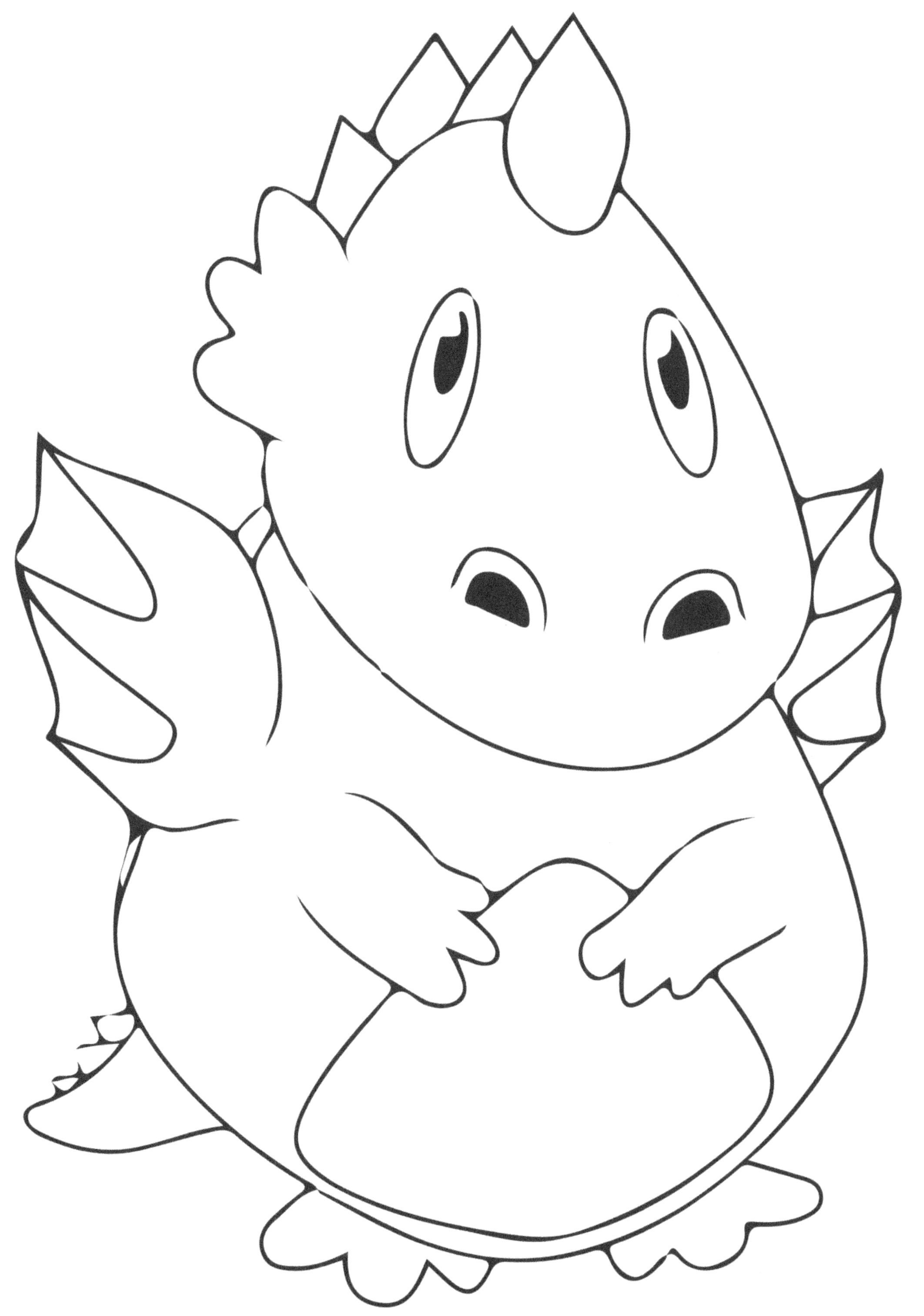

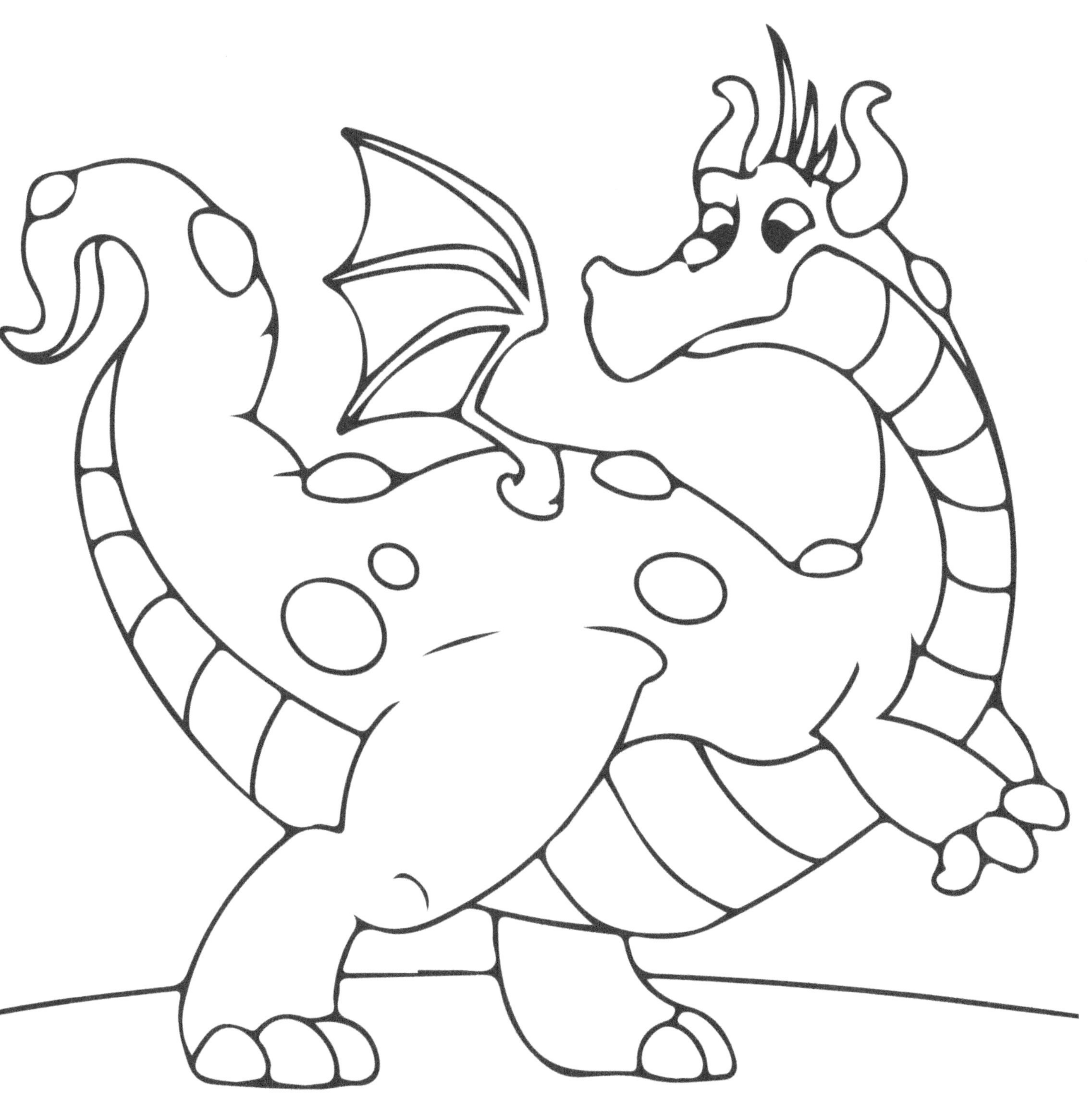

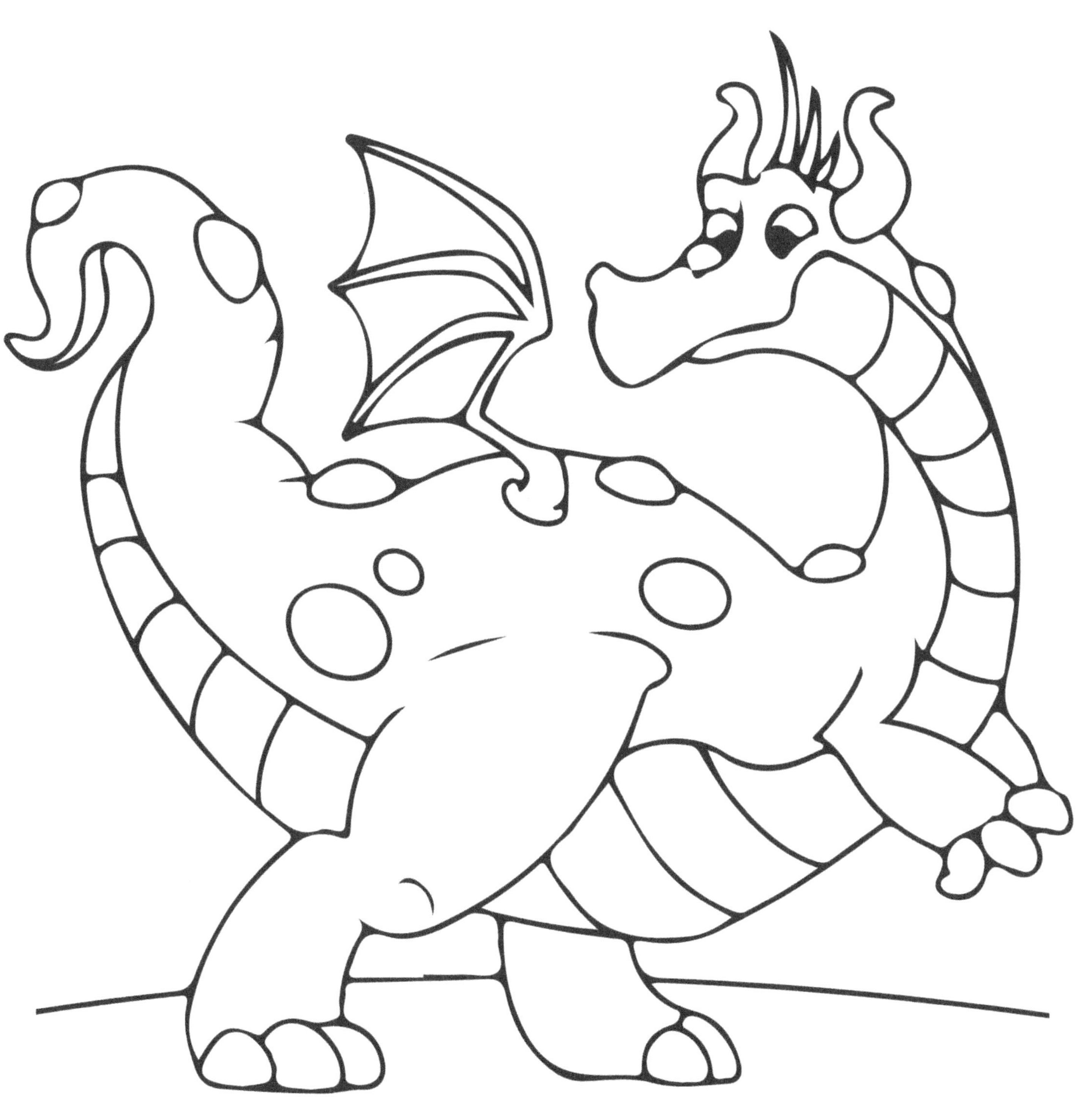

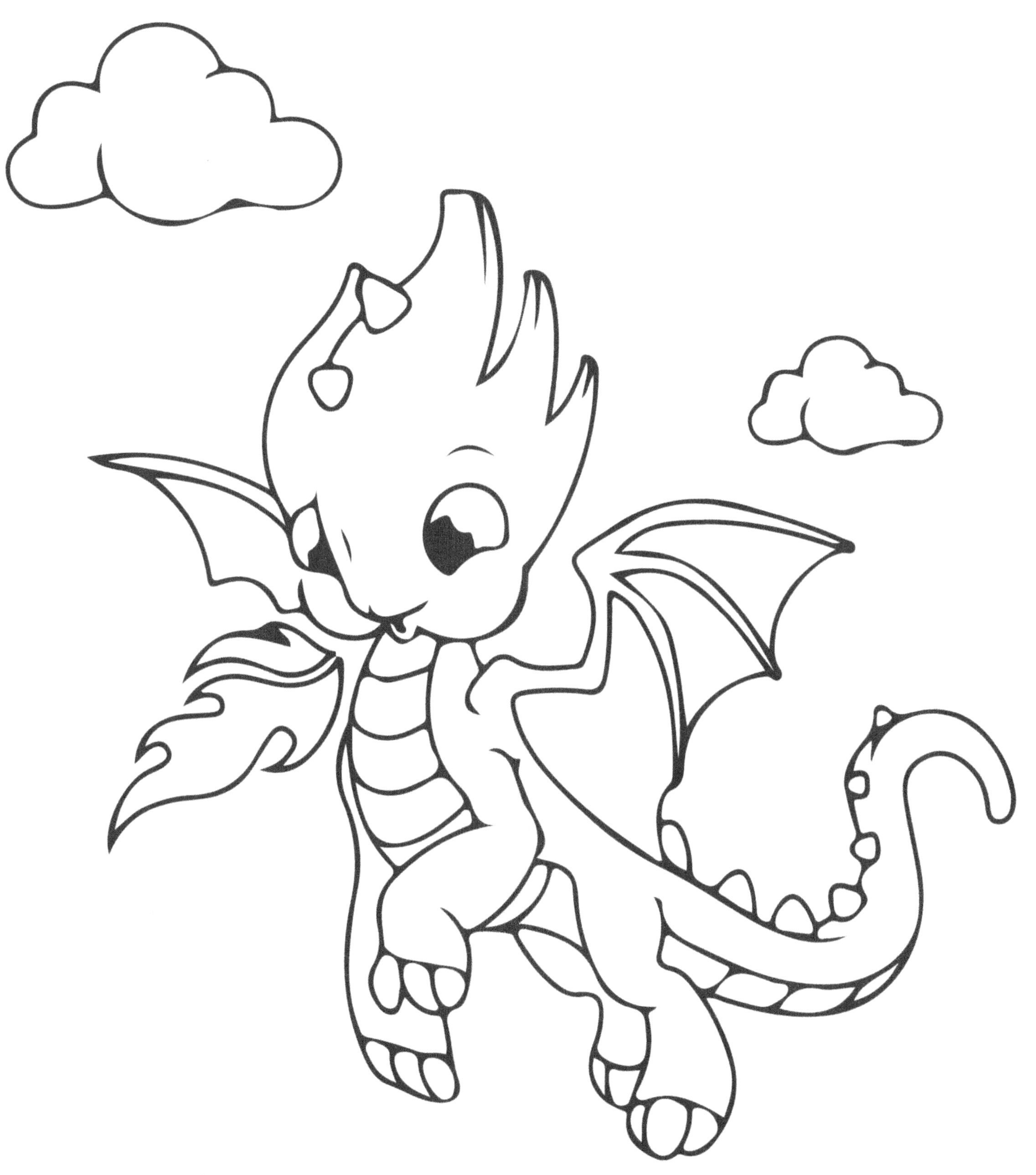

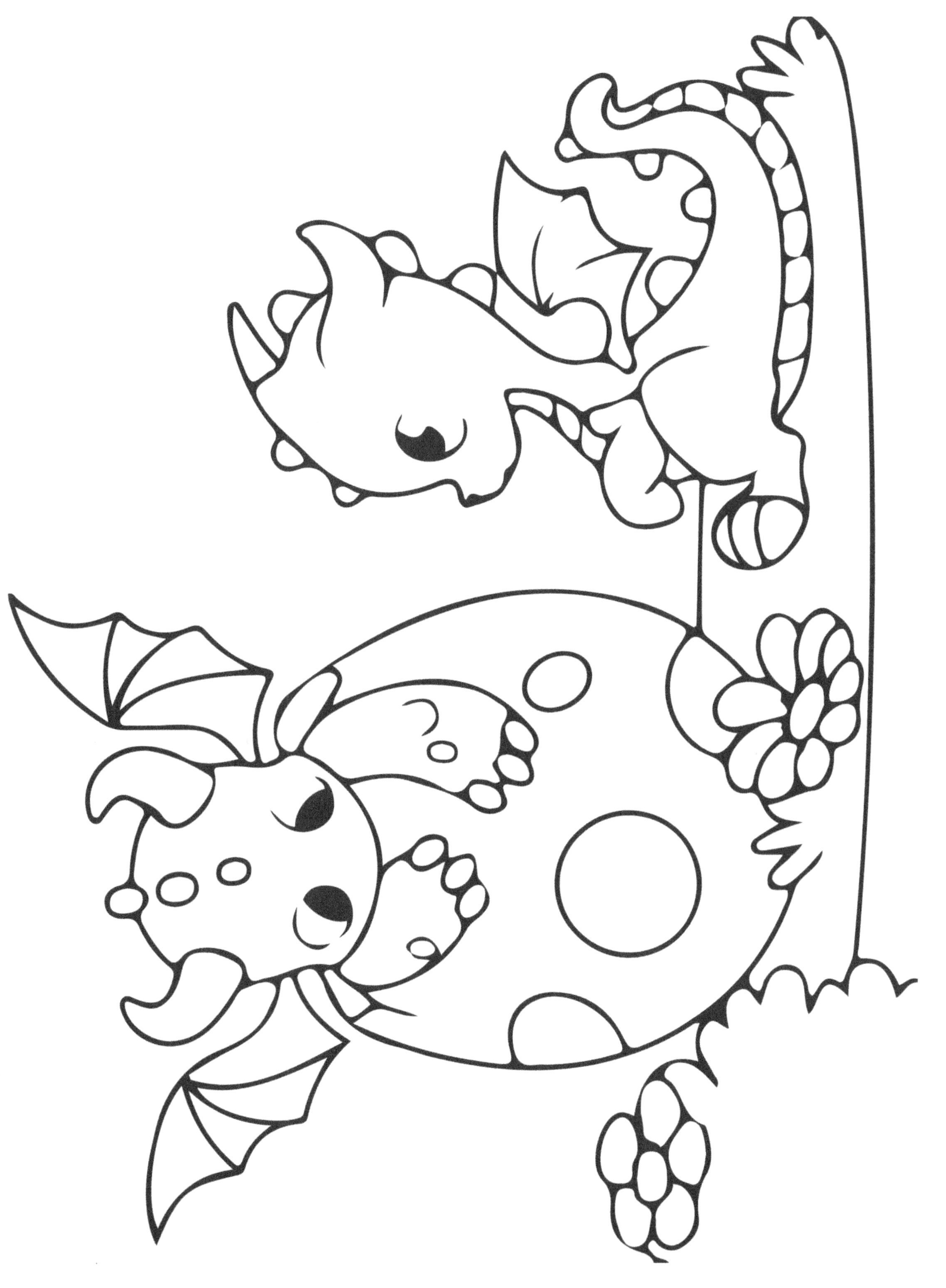

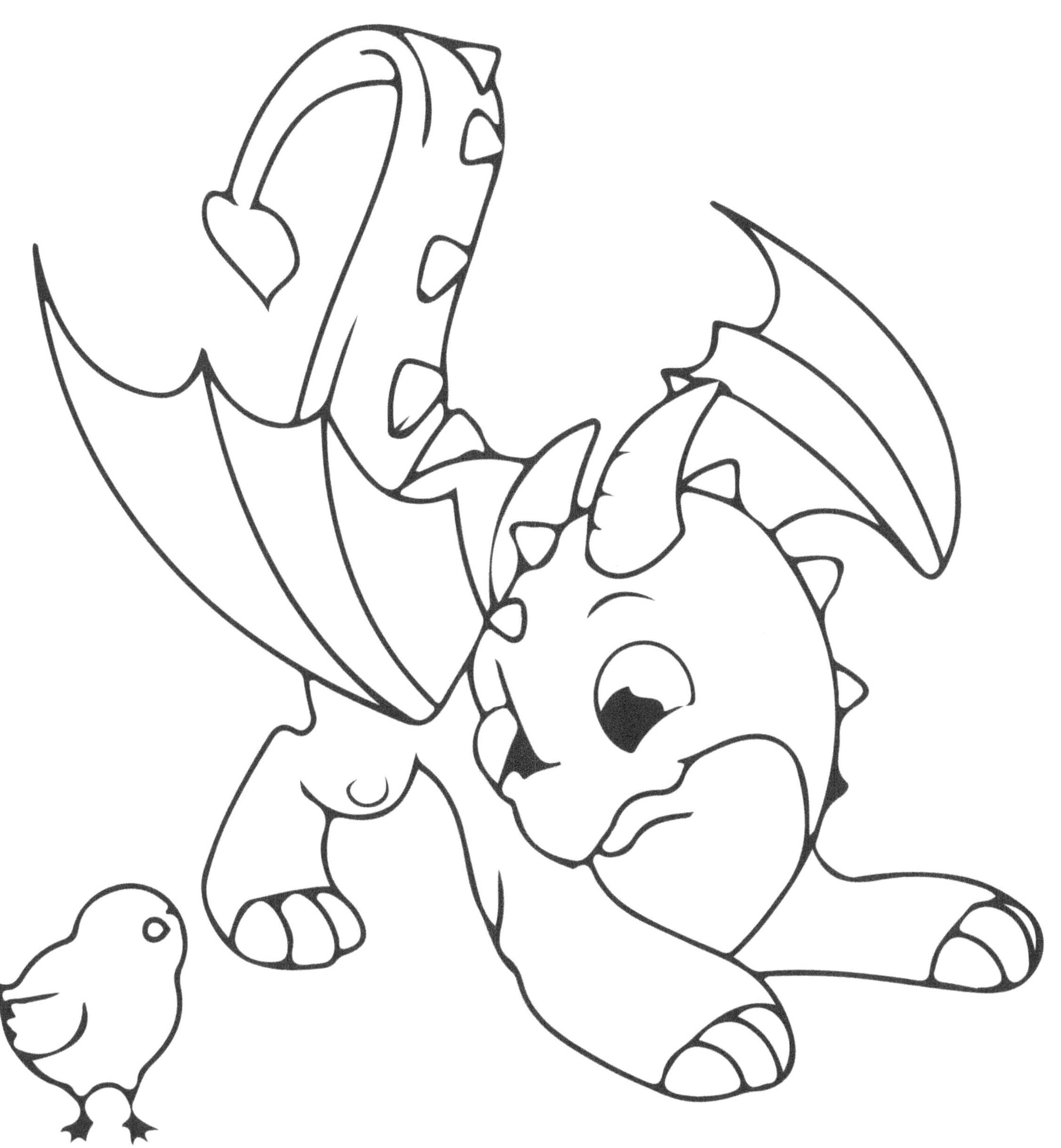

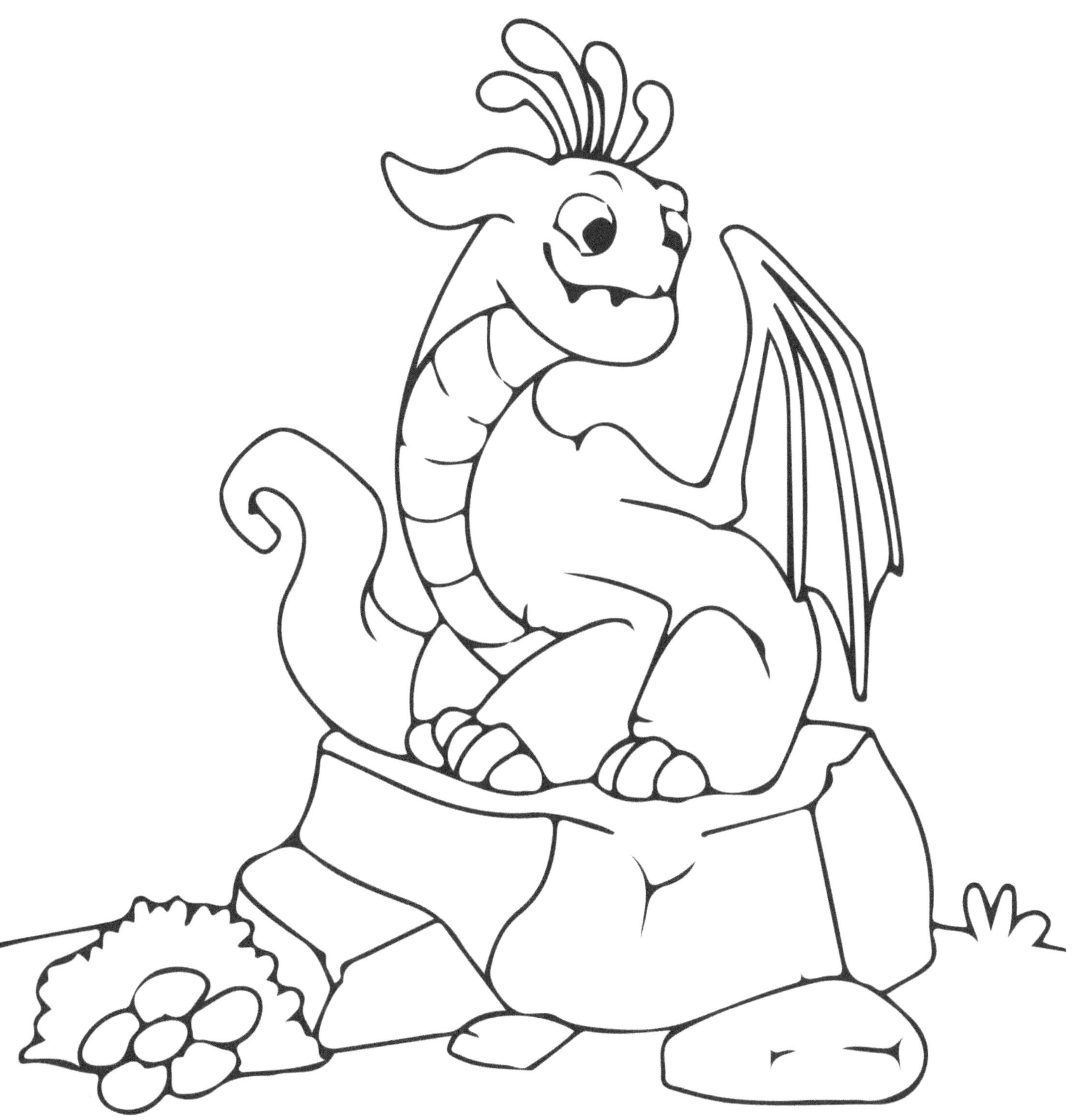

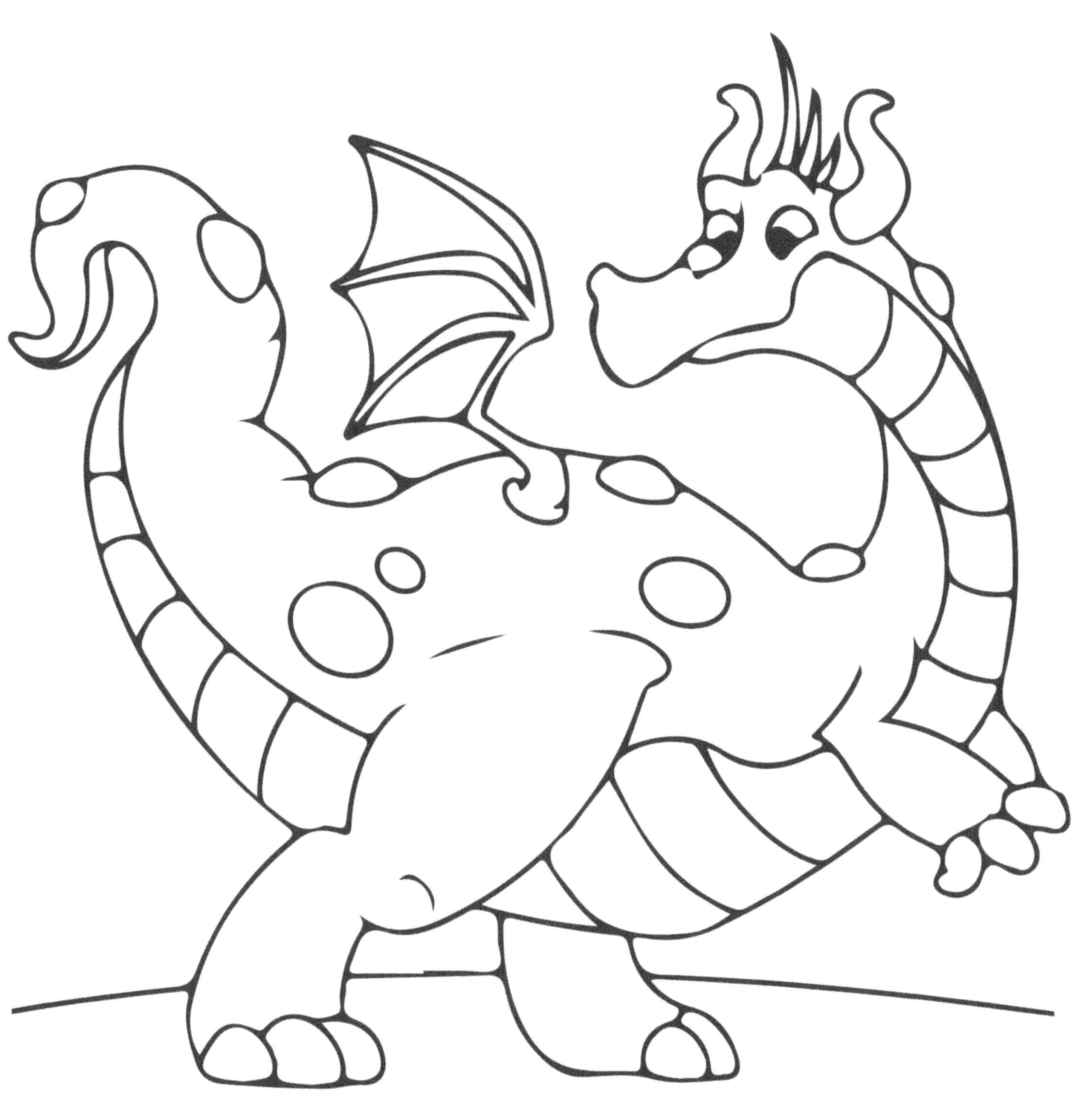

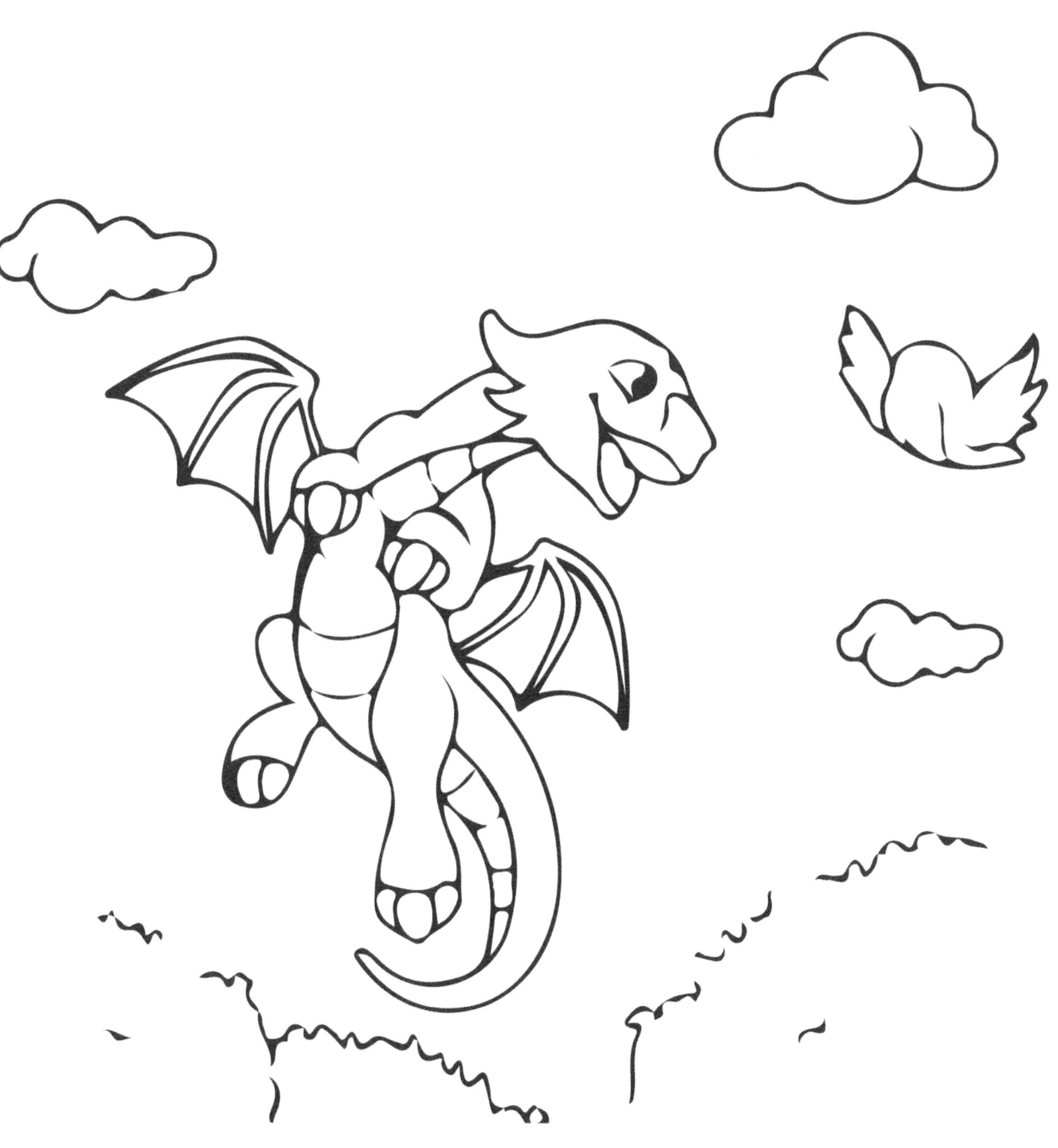

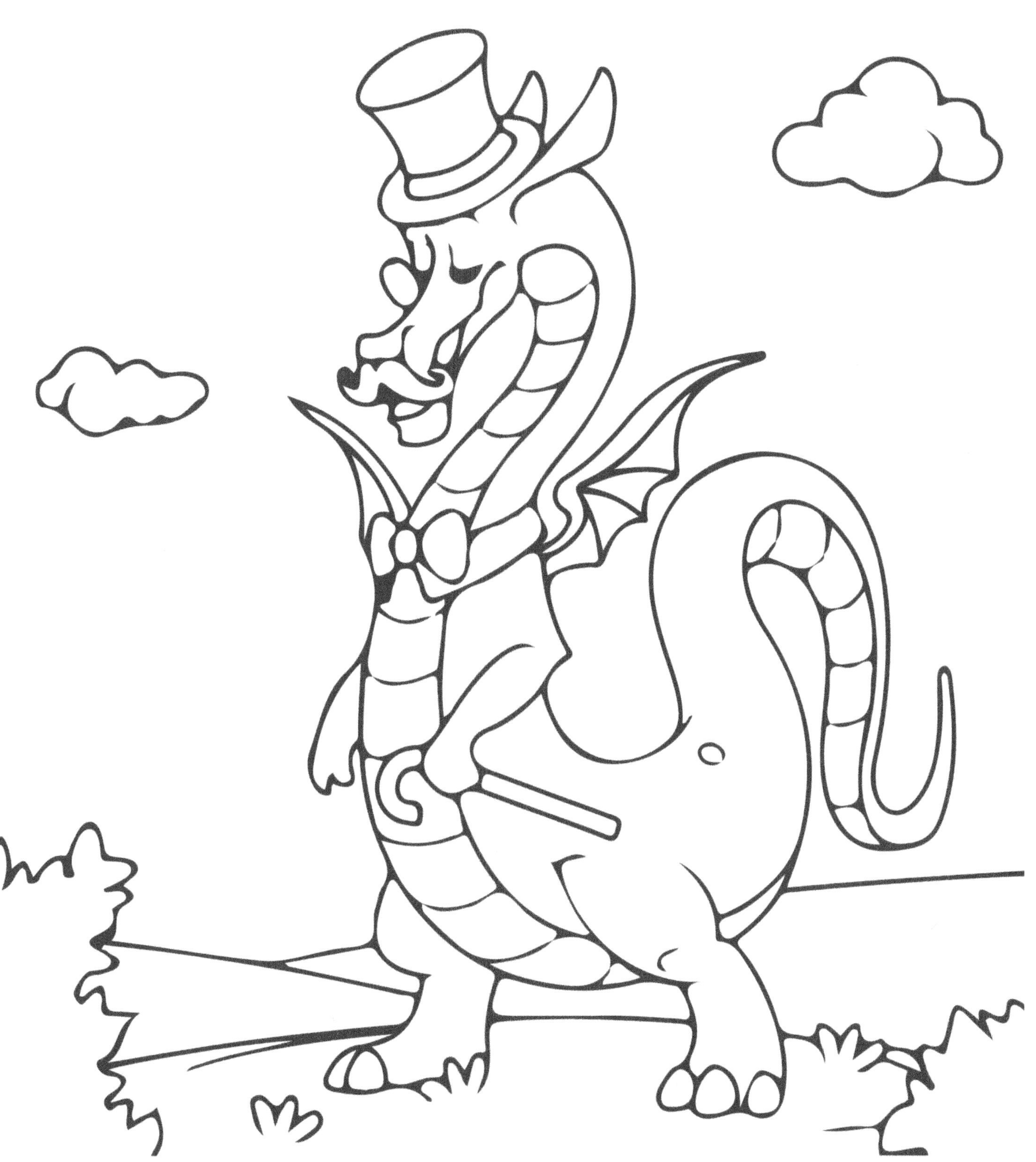

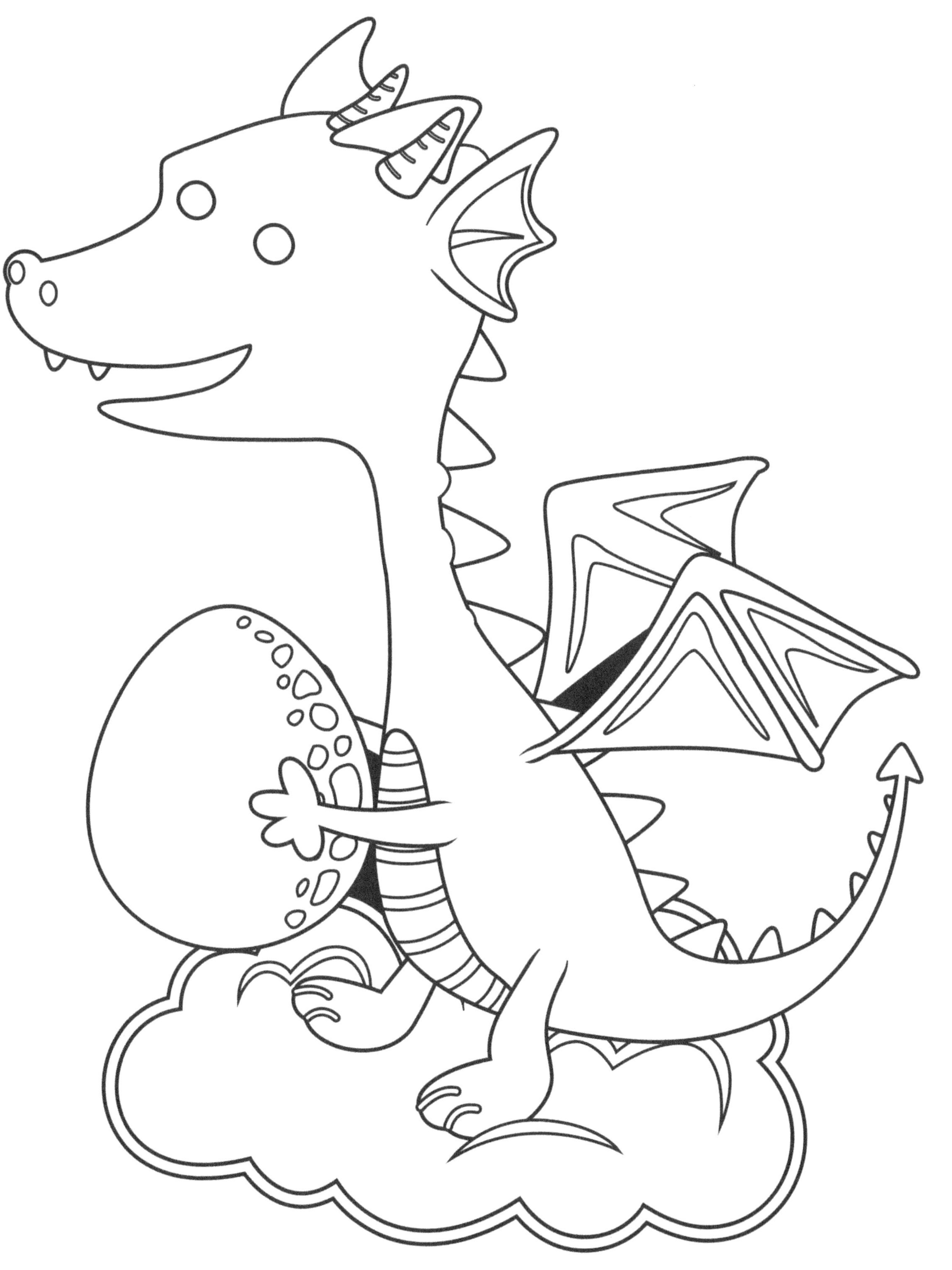

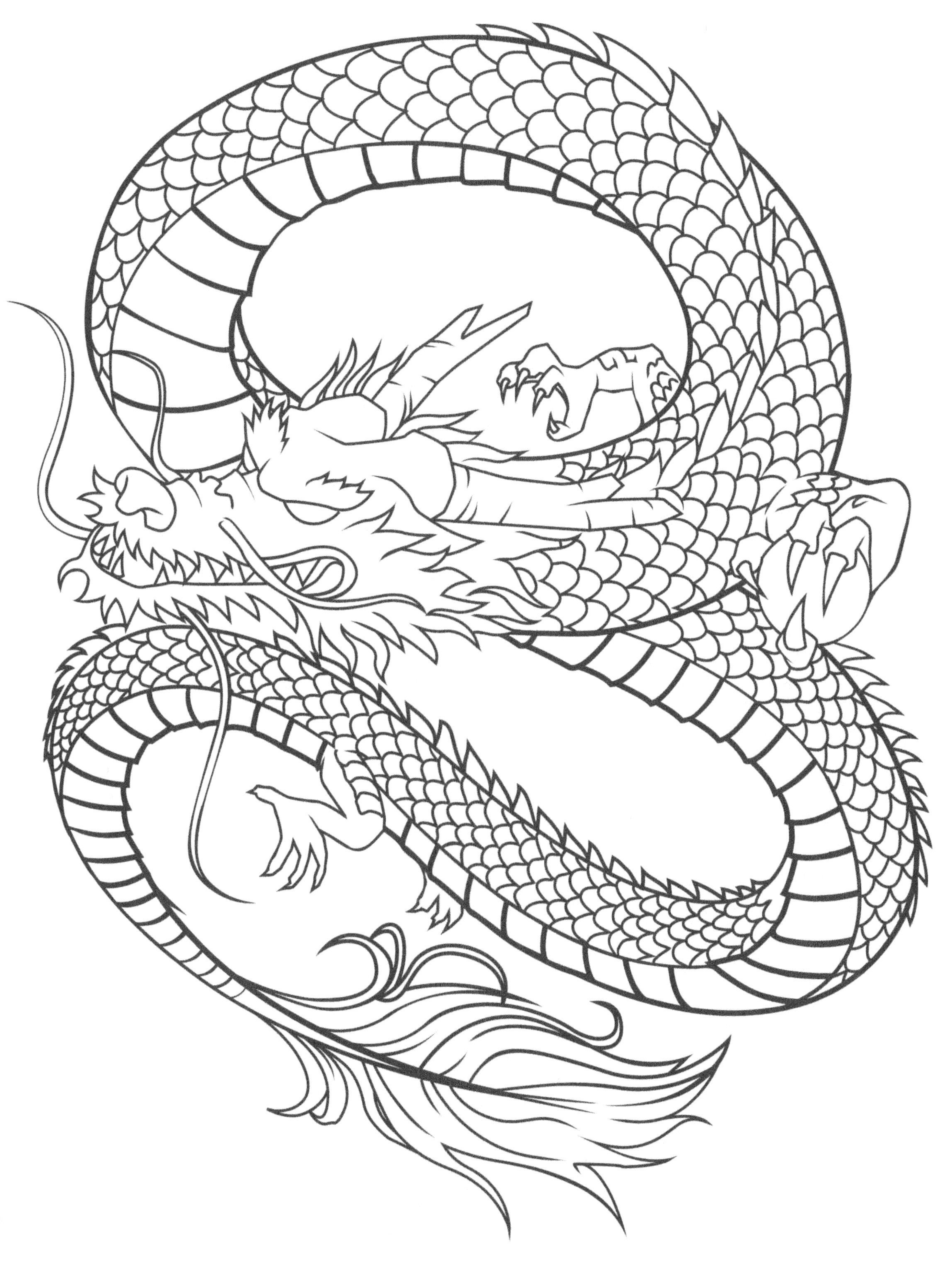

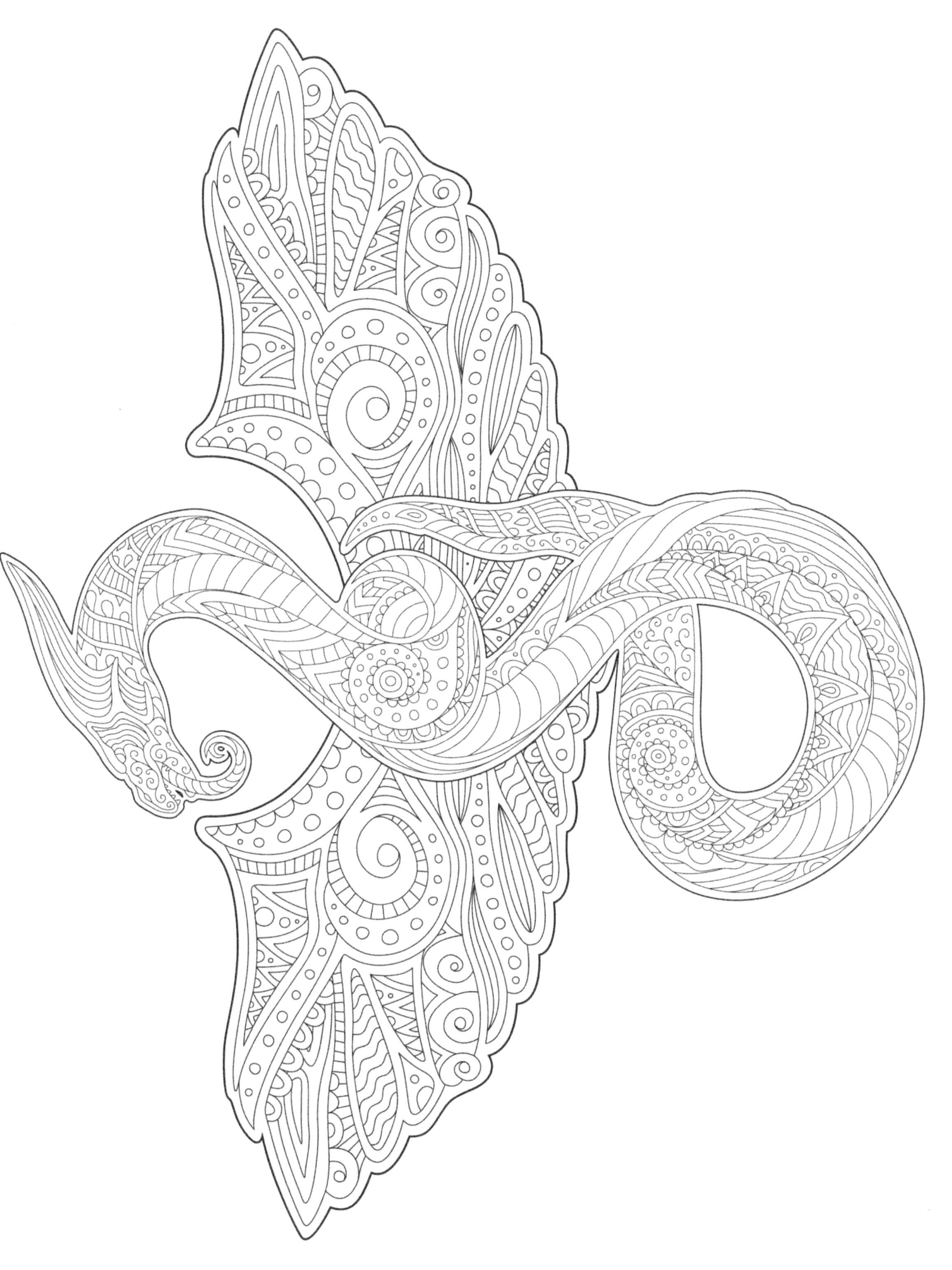

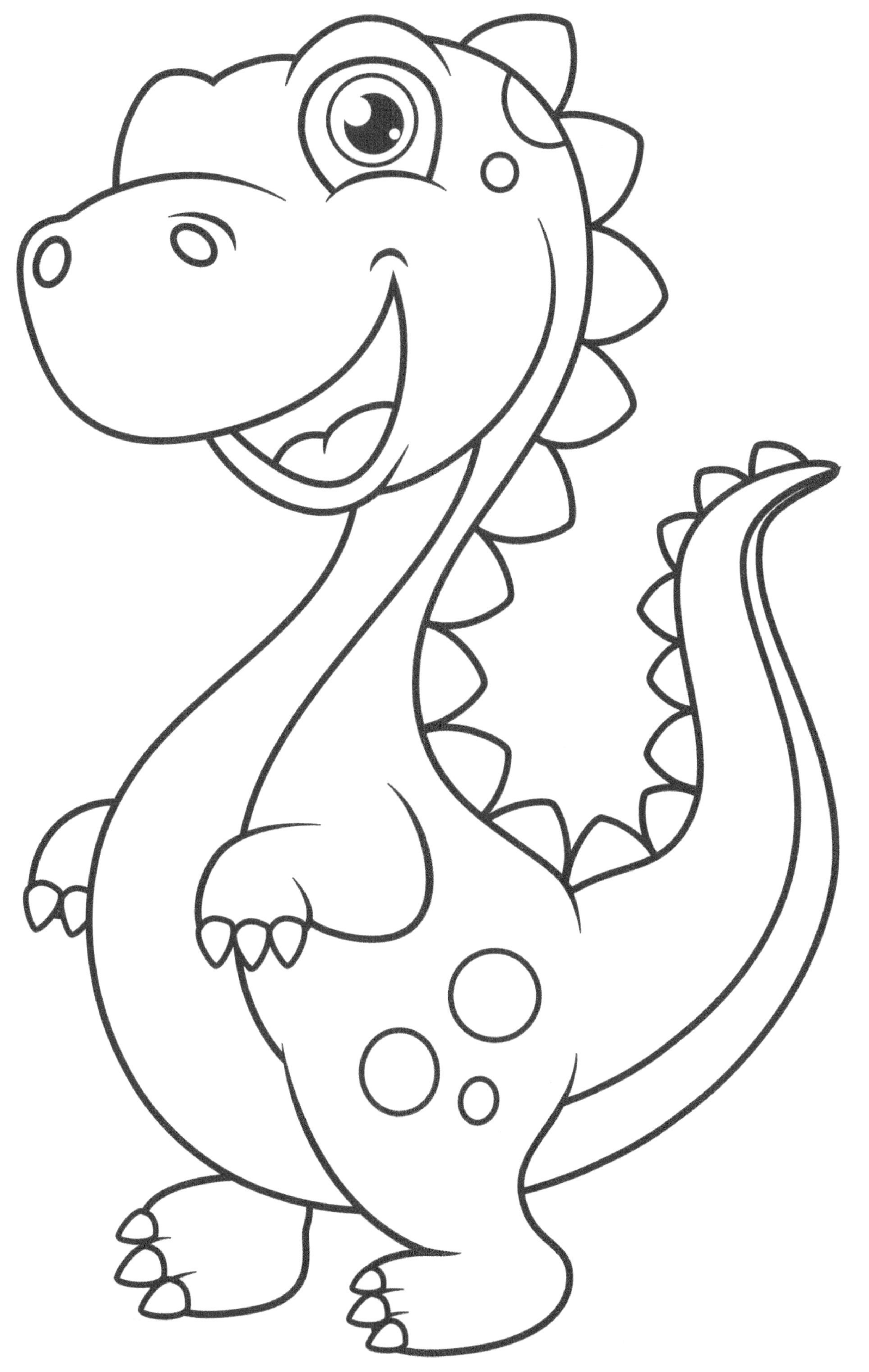

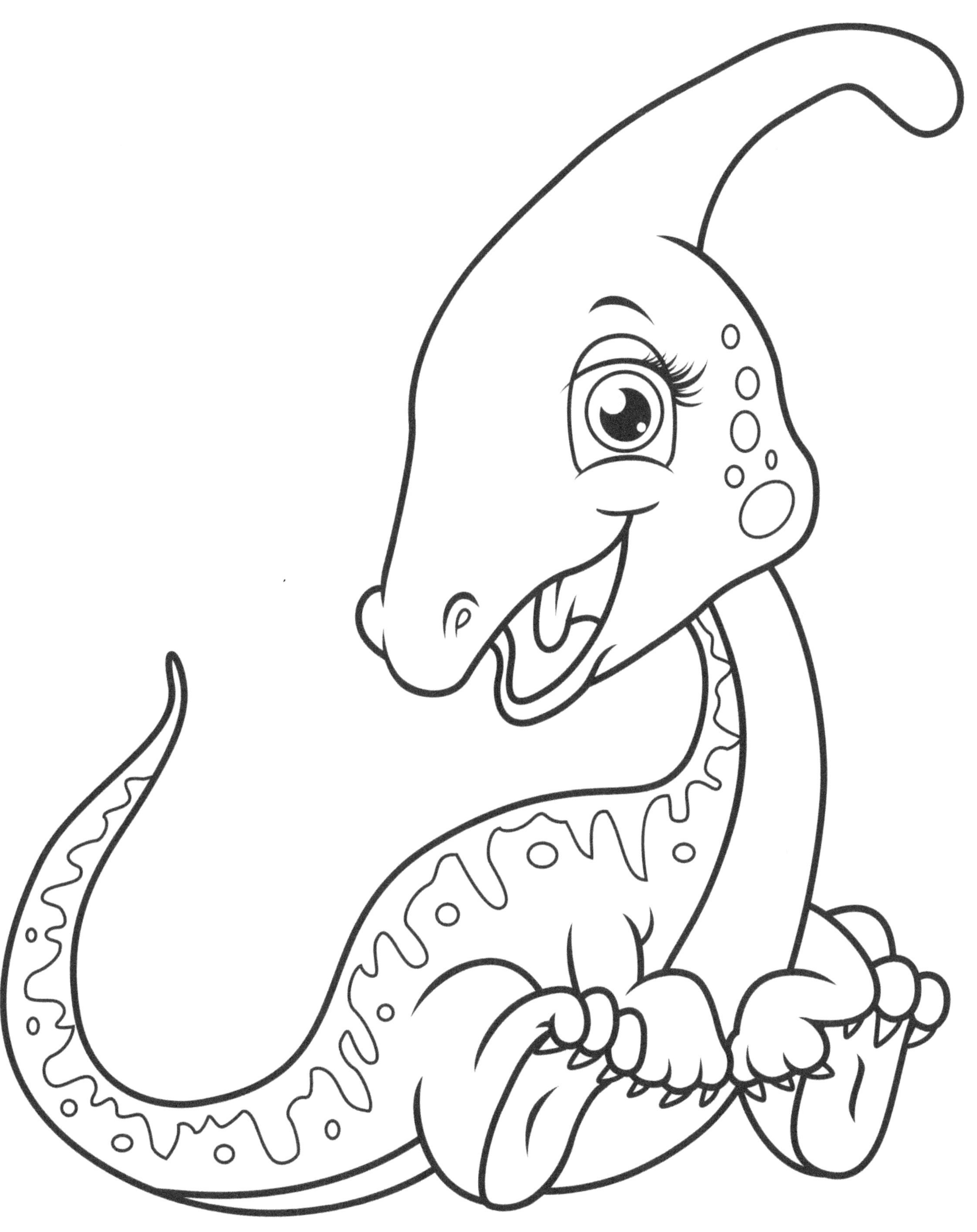

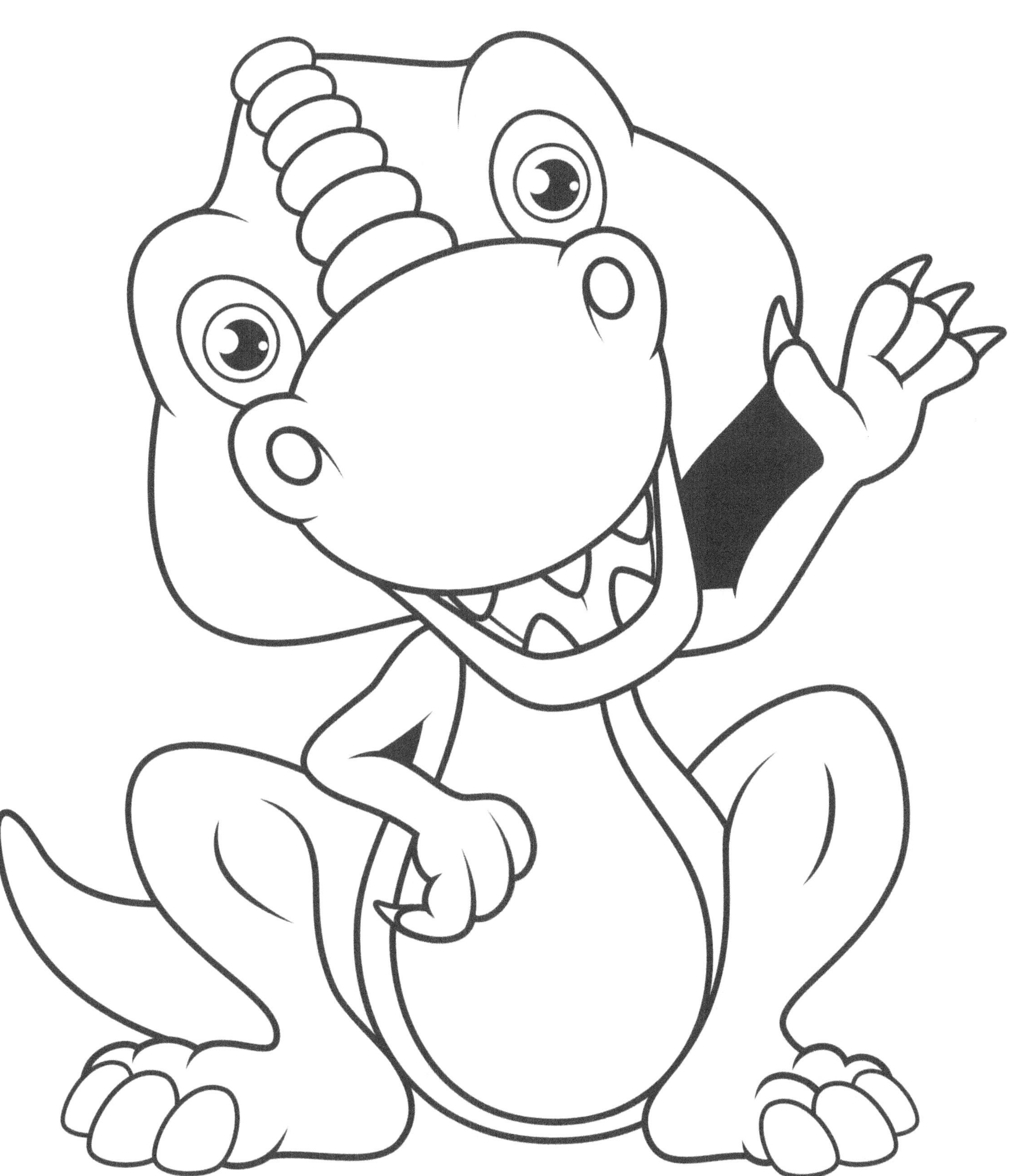